WEATHER AND CLIMATE

BARBARA TAYLOR

Kingfisher Books

NEW YORK

KINGFISHER BOOKS
Grisewood & Dempsey Inc.
95 Madison Avenue
New York, New York 10016

First American edition 1993
10 9 8 7 6 5 4 3 2
© Grisewood & Dempsey Ltd. 1992

Library of Congress
Cataloging-in-Publication Data
Taylor, Barbara
    Weather and climate / Barbara Taylor
— 1st American ed. p. cm.
    (Young discoverers) Includes index.
    Summary: An introduction to weather
and climate, discussing world climates,
seasons, violent weather, weather pollution,
and the elements of changing weather.
    1. Weather—Juvenile literature.
    2. Climatology—Juvenile literature.
    [1. Weather. 2. Climatology.] I. Title.
    II. Series: Taylor, Barbara Young
discoverers. QC981.T38 1993
551.5—dc20 92-28420 CIP AC

ISBN 1-85697-878-8 (lib. bdg.)
ISBN 1-85697-940-7 (pbk.)

Series editor: Sue Nicholson
Series and cover design: Terry Woodley
Design: Ben White
Picture research: Elaine Willis
Cover illustration: Chris Forsey
Illustrations: Kuo Kang Chen pp.2, 8-9 (bottom),
    11, 15 (top); David Evans, Kathy Jakeman
    Illustration p.26; Chris Forsey p.21; Hayward Art
    Group pp.6 (bottom right), 12 (top), 14 (top), 15
    (bottom), 24 (top), 28; Mike Lacey, Simon Girling
    & Associates p.17 (left); Kevin Maddison pp.4-5,
    10, 12, 13 (right), 14 (bottom), 22, 27, 28
    (top), 30-31; Maltings Partnership pp.7 (centre),
    9 (top), 17 (right), 19 (top and bottom right), 20
    (bottom), 22 (bottom left); Janos Marffy, Kathy
    Jakeman Illustration pp.6, 13, 16, 18-19, 23,
    25, 29, 31 (top); Clive Pritchard, Linden Artists
    pp.7, 8 (top), 24-25 (bottom); Simon Tegg,
    Simon Girling & Associates pp.6 (top), 18 (top);
    Stephen Walsh, Simon Girling & Associates p.20
Photographs: Hutchinson Library p.9; NASA p.5;
    NOAA p.27; Orion Press/ZEFA p.18; ZEFA
    pp.11, 16, 24, 26, 29, 30

Printed in Spain

About This Book

This book tells you about weather and weather patterns around the world. It also gives you lots of ideas for projects and things to look out for. You should be able to find nearly everything you need to do the projects around your home. You may need to buy some items, but they are all cheap and easy to find. Sometimes you will need to ask an adult to help you, such as when making some of the weather instruments.

Activity Hints

● Before you begin, read the instructions carefully and collect all the things you need.

● Put on some old clothes or wear an apron or coveralls.

● When you have finished, clear everything away, especially sharp things like knives and scissors.

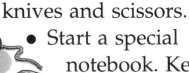

● Start a special notebook. Keep a record of what you do in each project and the things you find out.

Contents

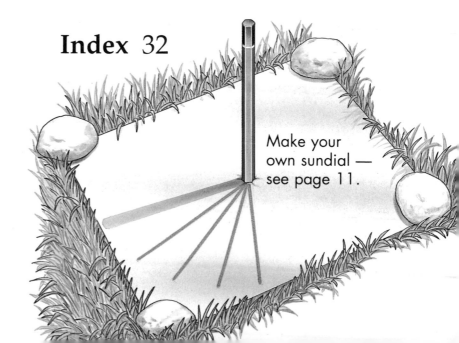

Make your own sundial — see page 11.

Weather on the Move

What's the weather like today? Is it sunny or cloudy, wet or dry, windy or still? In most parts of the world the weather is always changing. Weather changes are blown around the world by winds — movements in the air. Winds are formed when the Sun heats up some parts of the Earth more strongly than others, and the difference in heat makes the air move. Sometimes the weather can be very powerful, bringing violent storms or hurricanes.

Eye-Spy

Where you live, is the weather usually a little different every day? Start keeping a diary to record the changing weather.

When it is raining heavily, it can be unpleasant to go outside, but water is essential to life. Like all other animals, we need water to stay alive.

Scientists try to predict or forecast what the weather will be like the next day or over the next few days. This helps people to plan. For example, you would not want to go for a picnic in the countryside if the weather was going to be rainy and cold.

The weather forecast is very important to many people, particularly to those who work outdoors. For example, farmers need to decide when to plow their land and sow and harvest their crops.

The Atmosphere

Satellite photographs taken from space show a blue haze around the Earth. This is the air or the atmosphere. Weather occurs only in the lowest layer of the atmosphere, nearest Earth. Jet aircraft often fly above the clouds where the air is more still.

Weather Patterns

Although the weather may change every day, each part of the Earth has a usual pattern of weather that is the same over a long period of time. We call an area's usual weather pattern its climate.

Different areas of the Earth tend to have different types of climate — from hot and dry deserts to cold and snowy polar regions. An area's climate depends mainly on how close it is to the equator (an imaginary line around the middle of the Earth), its height, and how far it is from the sea.

City Climates

Cities are usually warmer than the countryside because building stone retains, or keeps in, the Sun's heat.

Do it yourself

Because the Earth's surface is curved, some areas receive more heat and light than others. Try the following experiment to see how this works.

Shine a flashlight onto an upright piece of cardboard. This is how the Sun's rays reach places on the equator, making them very hot. Now hold the card at an angle to see how the Sun's rays are more spread out near the Poles.

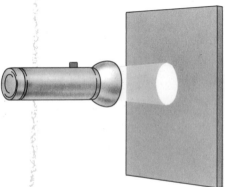

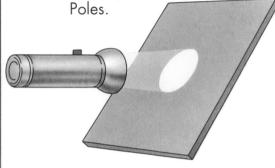

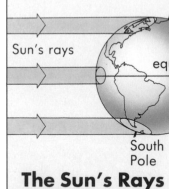

The Sun's Rays

At the Poles, the Sun's rays are more spread out so they have to heat a bigger area. This means the rays have less heating power, so climates are colder.

Polar and Tundra
Cold and dry all year round. Always icy at the Poles.

Cold Forests
Long snowy winters and short warm summers.

Temperate
Not too hot or too cold. Rainfall all year round.

Mountain
Cold and snowy on high peaks, warm on lowlands.

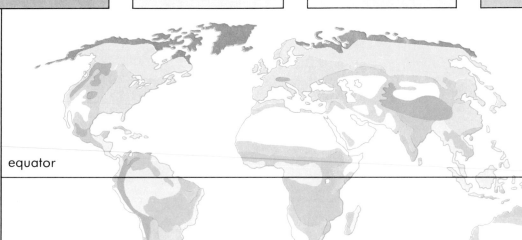

equator

Deserts
Very hot and dry all year, with hardly any rain.

Dry grasslands
Hot dry summers and cold snowy winters.

Tropical grasslands
Hot all year. Wet and dry seasons.

Rain forests
Hot and rainy all year round. Humid or steamy.

7

Seasons of the Year

In many parts of the world, the climate changes regularly throughout the year. These changes — spring, summer, autumn, and winter — are called seasons. They happen because of the way the Earth is tilted on its axis — an imaginary line between the North and South Poles. As the Earth slowly circles the Sun once every year, different parts of the Earth are closer to the Sun. This affects the amount of light and heat they receive. Look at the diagram on the opposite page to see how this works.

Winter Sleep
Some animals like this dormouse hibernate, or sleep, through the cold winter months. They live off stores of fat in their bodies until the spring.

Do it yourself

Make a model to see how the seasons work. You will need a table tennis ball, a straw, scissors, glue, colored pens, and a table lamp.

1. Cut the straw in half. Glue one half to the top of the ball and the other to the bottom. This is the Earth's axis.

2. Ask an adult to take the shade off a table lamp and switch on the lamp for you.

3. Walk slowly around the lamp, tilting your "Earth" at an angle and keeping it turned toward the Sun. See how the lamp lights up your Earth.

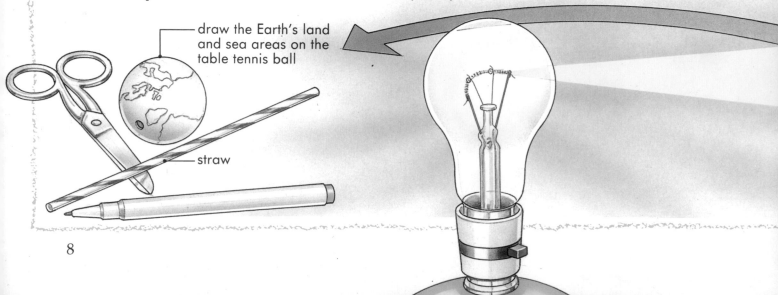

draw the Earth's land and sea areas on the table tennis ball

straw

How Seasons Work

When the North Pole is tilted toward the Sun (1), it is summer in the northern half of the world and winter in the southern half. Six months later, the South Pole leans toward the Sun (3), making it summer in the south and winter in the north.

During spring and autumn (2 and 4), the northern and southern parts of the Earth have more equal shares of the Sun's light. Areas near the equator have no real seasons because they are farthest from the Poles and are not affected by the tilt of the Earth.

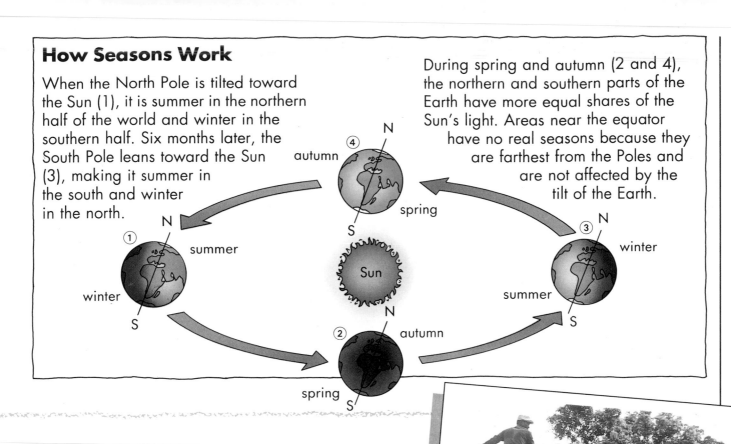

4. The Earth also spins on its axis once every 24 hours, giving us night and day. Try to turn your globe round and round at the same time to see how this works.

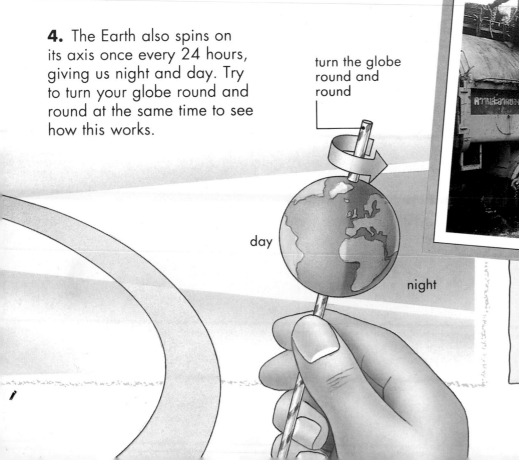

turn the globe round and round

day

night

Some tropical countries have a yearly rainy season called the monsoon. It may rain for days at a time and there can be severe floods.

Sun Power

Without the power of the Sun, there would be no weather. The Sun heats the land, which passes on some of this warmth to the air. This makes the air move because warm air rises. As the rising warm air moves farther away from the warm land, it cools and sinks. This is how air moves all over the world, causing winds that carry weather changes.

Hot air is lighter than cold air because it is more spread out — the same amount of air covers a bigger area. So hot air usually rises. Try blowing some bubbles over a hot radiator to see them float upward on the rising air.

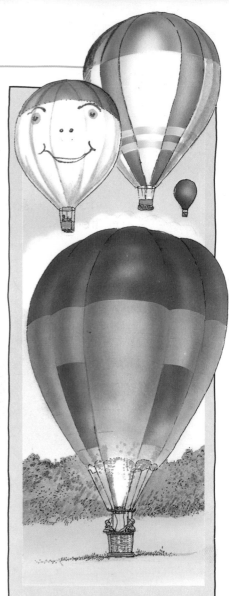

Hot Air Balloons

The air inside a hot air balloon is heated with a gas flame. As the hot air inside is lighter than the cooler air outside, the balloon floats upward. When the air inside cools down it gets heavier, so the balloon starts to sink.

Do it yourself

Make a sundial to tell the time. You will need a pencil and a piece of cardboard.

1. Build your sundial in a spot well away from trees and buildings — and don't forget to choose a sunny day!

2. Every hour, draw a line to mark the position of the pencil's shadow and write the time at the end of each line.

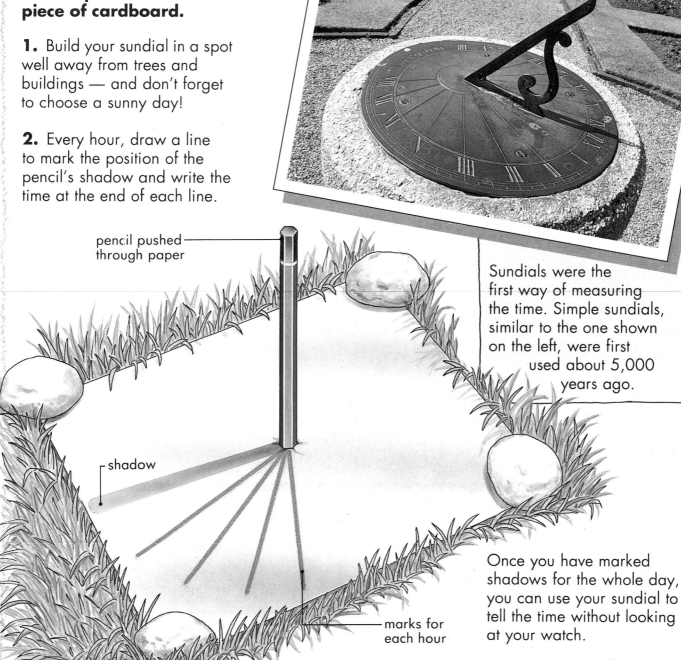

pencil pushed through paper

shadow

marks for each hour

Sundials were the first way of measuring the time. Simple sundials, similar to the one shown on the left, were first used about 5,000 years ago.

Once you have marked shadows for the whole day, you can use your sundial to tell the time without looking at your watch.

11

Heat and Cold

Changes in the weather are caused by changes in temperature — how hot or cold the air is. So it is important to be able to measure temperature accurately. We can do this with a thermometer. Most thermometers consist of a long thin tube containing a liquid such as mercury or alcohol, which is sensitive to changes in temperature. When the liquids become warm they expand or take up more space, and move up the tube. We then read off the temperature from the scale beside the tube.

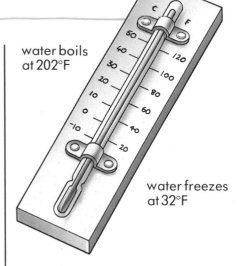

water boils at 202°F

water freezes at 32°F

Temperature is usually measured in degrees Fahrenheit (°F) or Celsius (°C). These temperature scales are based on the point at which water boils and freezes.

Sea Breezes

On a hot day at the beach, there is often a cool breeze — a sea breeze — blowing. This happens because the land heats up more quickly than the sea, warming the air above it. The warm air rises and cool air from the sea blows in to take its place.

At night, the land cools more quickly than the sea, cooling the air above. The cool air blows out to sea, under rising warmer air. This is called a land breeze.

Do it yourself

Make your own simple thermometer using a strong plastic bottle with a screw cap, a thin plastic straw, modeling clay, tape, and thick cardboard. Color the water with poster paint.

1. Ask an adult to drill a hole in the bottle's cap. Assemble the thermometer, making sure that the water comes part way up the straw when you fix on the cap. Leave the water to settle for an hour then mark the water level on the scale.

cold water

hot water

2. Stand the thermometer in a bowl of ice cold water and a bowl of very hot water. See how the water level changes.

hole through screw cap

scale drawn on piece of cardboard

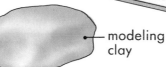

modeling clay

plastic straw

Air Temperature

Ask an adult to help you fix a thermometer in a shady, dry place outdoors. Keep a record of the daily temperature for a month.

13

Air Pressure

When you take off or land in an aircraft, your ears may hurt or feel uncomfortable. This is because your eardrums can feel changes in air pressure as the aircraft moves quickly up and down. But what is air pressure? It is caused by the weight of all the air in the atmosphere pressing down on Earth. Air pressure changes with height and also when air warms up or cools down. Changes in air pressure cause changes in the weather.

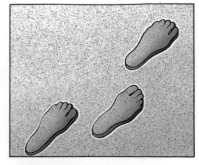

👁 Eye Spy

We do not usually notice air pressure because of the air inside us. This presses outward and cancels out the air pressure that presses all around us from outside. But you can see the effect of pressure from the weight of your body on a beach, when your footsteps sink in wet sand!

At the top of very high mountains, the air pressure is low. This is because the air that surrounds the Earth gets thinner the higher you go.

Do it yourself

Try this experiment to see the effect of air pressure.

1. Fill a glass with water up to the brim then place a piece of cardboard over the top.

2. Keep your hand on the card and turn the glass upside down.

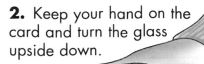

flip the glass upside down.

glass full of water

thick cardboard

3. Now take your hand away — the air pressing up against the cardboard stops the water falling out of the glass. Air pressure is very powerful even though we cannot see it.

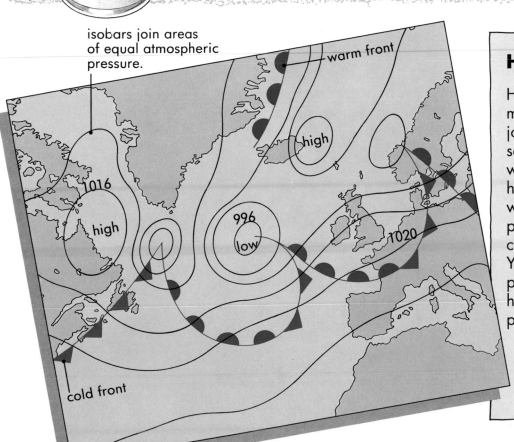

isobars join areas of equal atmospheric pressure.

warm front

high

1016

high

996 low

1020

cold front

Highs and Lows

Here is a simple weather map. Lines called isobars join up places with the same air pressure. Areas with high pressure usually have fine, settled weather while those with low pressure usually have cloudy, rainy weather. You can find out why on pages 20-21. Cold fronts happen when cold air pushes under warm air. Warm fronts happen when warm air slides up over cold air.

Do it yourself

Air pressure is measured with an instrument called a barometer. Try making your own simple barometer.

1. Cut a small piece from a balloon, stretch it over the top of a plastic container and secure it with a rubber band.

2. Tape the straw to the middle of the balloon.

3. Mark a scale on a piece of cardboard and fix it beside your barometer.

4. Check your barometer at the same time each day and mark where the straw comes to on the scale. Changes in air pressure will make the balloon and straw move slightly up and down.

Above: We measure air pressure to find out when the weather is about to change. Another way is to watch clouds, as clouds often form in areas of low pressure. See page 21 for some cloud-watching tips.

scale drawn on piece of cardboard

balloon

rubber band

tape

plastic container

straw

(high pressure— straw moves up; low pressure— straw moves down)

Windy Weather

When the wind blows, it is rather like letting air out of a balloon. The air inside the balloon is at high pressure and it rushes out to where the pressure is lower. Winds all over the world are caused by differences in temperature and pressure, and they always blow from high to low pressure areas. Some winds that blow regularly in just one area have a special name, like the cold Mistral wind in southern France. Other winds sweep across the whole Earth.

Thousands of years ago, the Chinese flew kites to frighten their enemies or to measure the power of the wind. Today, we fly kites mainly for fun.

Right: The Beaufort Scale is used to describe wind strength. It has 12 numbers, ranging from calm to a violent storm or hurricane.

1 smoke drifts

2 leaves rustle

3 flags flap

4 paper blows

5 small waves on water

6 umbrellas blow inside out

7 hard to walk

8 9 tiles blown off roofs

10 11 trees uprooted

12 buildings destroyed

Windy Weather

The two most important things about the wind are its strength or speed and the direction in which it is blowing. We use a weather vane or a windsock (a kind of long cloth tube through which the wind is funneled) to see wind direction. Wind strength is measured by the Beaufort Scale, windsocks, or by special scientific instruments called anemometers. These machines have several small cups that spin when caught in the wind. The speed of the spin is then measured against a scale.

The "tower of the winds" was built 2,000 years ago in Athens, Greece. It shows eight gods or spirits dressed to suit different winds.

Gaily colored banners are used at festivals in Japan. These tube-shaped banners flutter and flap in the wind rather like windsocks.

Do it yourself

Make your own weather vane to find out the wind direction.

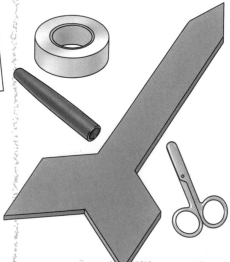

1. Cut out an arrow from thick cardboard and tape a pen top to its middle.

2. Fix a knitting needle or a wooden stick to a heavy base, such as a brick, so that it does not move. Slide the pen top and arrow over it.

3. Put your weather vane outside where it will catch the wind. Remember that the arrow will point in the direction the wind is blowing *from*. Ask an adult to help you check the wind directions with a compass.

Wind Direction

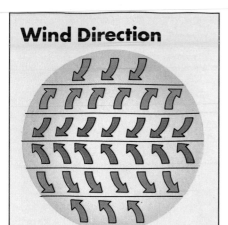

Because the Earth spins on its axis, global winds curve rather than blowing in straight lines from north to south.

The fastest sailing ships to carry cargo were called clippers. Clippers depended on powerful global winds called trade winds to carry them from China to the West. The ships used to race each other to break new speed records and be the first to deliver their cargoes.

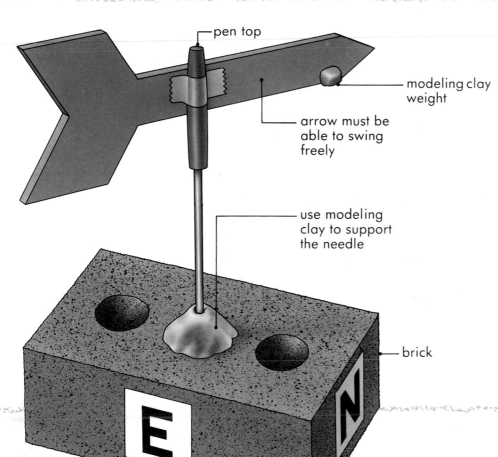

pen top

modeling clay weight

arrow must be able to swing freely

use modeling clay to support the needle

brick

E

N

Below: Make a wind rose to record the direction of the wind. Color a strip when the wind blows from one direction. Is there a main, or prevailing, wind in your area?

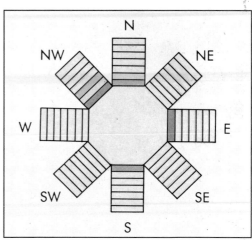

N

NW

NE

W

E

SW

SE

S

Cloudy Skies

Clouds are formed when warm air rises or when warm and cold air meet. Clouds are made up of billions of tiny droplets of water or ice. All air contains some water. Near the ground, this is usually in the form of an invisible gas called water vapor. But when air rises, it cools down. Cool air cannot hold as much water vapor as warm air, so some of the vapor turns into drops of liquid water. This liquid water then collects to form clouds. The process of water turning from a gas into a liquid is called condensation.

Eye-Spy

Steam forms in the same way as clouds, when moist, warm air rises and condenses as it meets cooler air.

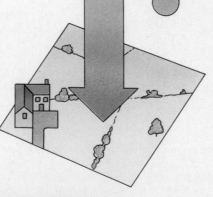

Low Pressure

In a low pressure area, warm air rises and cools. The moisture in the air condenses and clouds are formed, bringing rain.

High Pressure

In a high pressure area, cool air sinks, becoming warmer and drier as it nears the ground. This brings fine, settled weather.

There are three main cloud groups. The highest, called cirrus, are usually made of ice crystals because the air is so cold. White, fluffy piles of clouds are called cumulus, meaning "heap." Sometimes they join together to form huge, towering storm clouds, called cumulonimbus. Flat clouds are called stratus, meaning "layer." Fog is a low-lying stratus cloud.

20

cirrus

altostratus

cumulus

cumulonimbus

stratus

Cloud Watching

Look at the shape, size, and height of clouds to predict what the weather will be like.

Cumulus clouds usually mean fine weather while cirrus clouds tell us that the weather is about to change.

Rainy Days

Raindrops form inside clouds as billions of tiny water droplets bump into each other, joining up to form bigger, heavier droplets. Eventually, the droplets become so heavy they cannot float in the air, so they fall out of the clouds as rain.

Every raindrop is made up of about a million cloud droplets. The rain that falls from clouds eventually returns to the air as water vapor. This makes up part of the never-ending cycle that we call the water cycle.

It's Raining Frogs!

Rain clouds sometimes carry other things than water — strong winds have swept up fish and frogs!

How Raindrops Form

Raindrops form inside clouds when tiny water droplets stick together or when ice crystals warm up and melt into droplets.

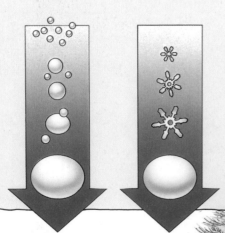

A rainbow may form when sunlight shines through raindrops — the drops split up the seven colors that make up sunlight.

Do it yourself

Try making a rain detector that will set off an alarm when it starts to rain. You will need a plastic bottle or tube, tape, glue, sugar cubes, and some marbles.

1. Rest a tray or a board on a brick to make a slope.

2. Glue a row of sugar lumps near the top of the board.

3. Put some marbles in the container, seal the end with tape, and rest it on the sugar lumps.

4. When it rains, the sugar cubes will dissolve in the water and the container will roll noisily down the slope.

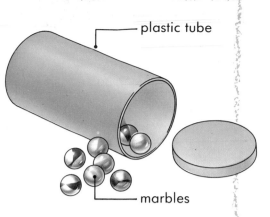

plastic tube

marbles

prop up the board on a brick

sugar lumps

Collecting Rainfall

Make a simple rain gauge to record rainfall.

1. Cut an old plastic bottle in half and turn the top upside down to make a funnel.

2. Make a scale and tape it to the side of the bottle.

3. Keep a daily record of how much rainfall you collect over several weeks or even months, and make a chart of your findings.

top of a plastic bottle

Ice and Snow

If the air in a cloud is below freezing, or 32°F (0°C), some of the water vapor freezes into ice crystals instead of forming water droplets. These crystals stick together to make snowflakes. The shape of a snowflake depends on the temperature and the amount of water in a cloud. Needle-shaped flakes form in very cold moist air, while star shapes form in warmer air.

When snowflakes are heavy enough, they fall out of the cloud as snow. Sometimes they melt before they reach the ground.

Every snowflake has six points, but each snowflake has a different shape.

Snow acts like a comforter on a bed, trapping tiny pockets of air which keep in heat. Small animals can move around in tunnels under the snow.

Heavy snow can build up behind walls and fences to form deep drifts — even burying cars!

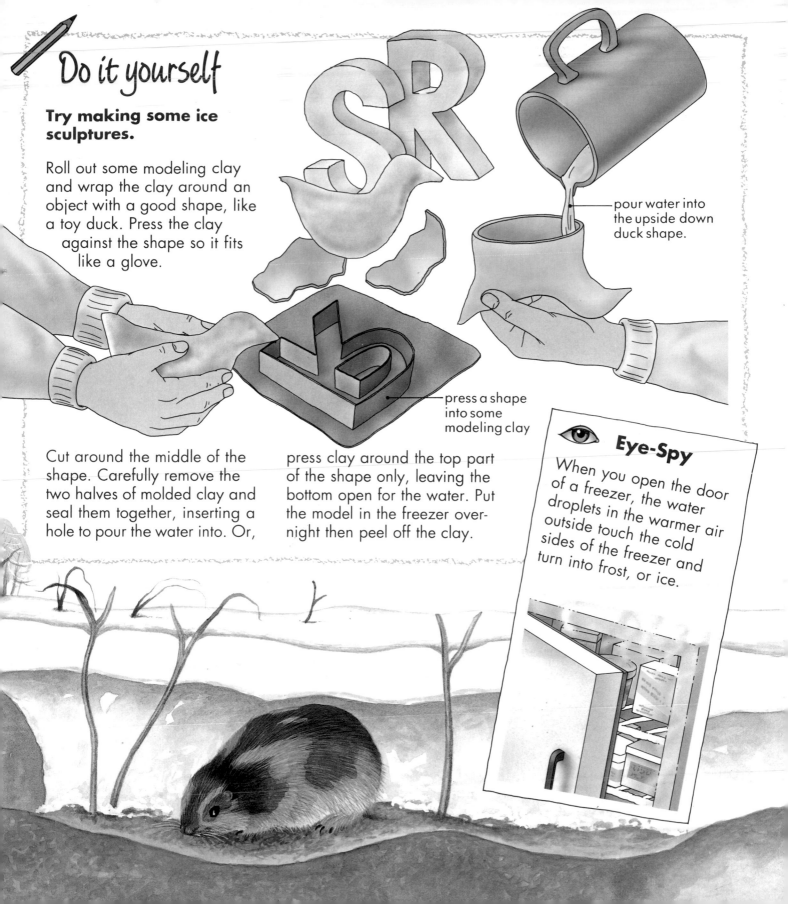

Do it yourself

Try making some ice sculptures.

Roll out some modeling clay and wrap the clay around an object with a good shape, like a toy duck. Press the clay against the shape so it fits like a glove.

pour water into the upside down duck shape.

press a shape into some modeling clay

Cut around the middle of the shape. Carefully remove the two halves of molded clay and seal them together, inserting a hole to pour the water into. Or,

press clay around the top part of the shape only, leaving the bottom open for the water. Put the model in the freezer overnight then peel off the clay.

Eye-Spy

When you open the door of a freezer, the water droplets in the warmer air outside touch the cold sides of the freezer and turn into frost, or ice.

Violent Weather

Violent, stormy weather can be very dangerous, causing great damage and even injuring or killing people and wildlife. As we discover more about the weather, it becomes easier to forecast violent storms and avoid disasters.

Hurricanes and tornadoes form in warm, damp air when winds hurl into each other from opposite directions. Hurricanes grow over oceans, while tornadoes form over land. Hurricanes are sometimes called typhoons or tropical cyclones.

👁 Eye-Spy

If you rub a balloon on your sweater it will stick to the wall because it becomes charged with static electricity — like lightning.

How Far is the Storm?

Thunderstorms happen when warm moist air rises quickly, forming tall dark cumulo-nimbus clouds. Electric charges build up in the clouds, sparking down to the ground as lightning flashes. The lightning heats the air, making it explode with a crash of thunder. You can work out how many miles away a storm is by counting the seconds between the flash and the thunder then dividing by five. So if you count five seconds, the storm is a mile away.

Right: On this satellite photograph you can see a hurricane's swirling circular clouds that bring torrential rain. In the middle of the storm is a circle where the air is calm and still. This is often called the "eye" of the storm.

Tornado Facts

- Tornadoes or "twisters" are whirling funnels of air that form between the bottom of a storm cloud and the ground.
- Tornadoes last from 15 minutes to 5 hours.
- Some tornadoes can lift heavy objects like trucks right off the ground.
- In the United States, there are about 700 tornadoes every year.
- The word "tornado" comes from *tronada*, the Spanish word for thunderstorm.

Changing the Weather

Our climate has changed many times since Earth was formed millions of years ago. However, the pollution caused by people may be changing the climate much faster than it would change naturally. One of these changes is called the greenhouse effect. This is a warming of the Earth's climate by some gases that act like the glass windows of a greenhouse, trapping heat inside the atmosphere. Greenhouse gases include carbon dioxide, which is produced when fuels like coal, oil, and gas are burned.

Some scientists believe that the dinosaurs died out when the Earth's climate grew cooler and it became too cold for the dinosaurs to survive.

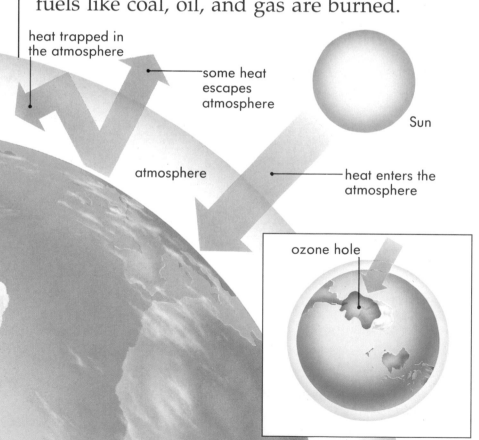

heat trapped in the atmosphere

some heat escapes atmosphere

Sun

atmosphere

heat enters the atmosphere

ozone hole

Ozone Holes

Ozone is a type of gas. It forms a layer in the atmosphere, shielding Earth from the Sun's ultra-violet light rays. These rays give us suntans but too much ultraviolet light can harm our skins.

Over the North and South Poles, the ozone layer has become very thin. It is being damaged by chemicals called CFCs (for chlorofluorocarbons), which are found in plastic packaging and cooling systems in refrigerators.

Do it yourself

glass jar

Test out the greenhouse effect to see how it works.

Place two thermometers in the sun but cover one with a glass jar. Leave them for an hour then check the temperature of each to see which is higher.

Keep a scrapbook of clippings from newspapers and magazines about pollution. Look out for articles on the greenhouse effect, ozone holes, and acid rain. What are the latest theories and developments?

What You Can Do

- Power stations burn coal and oil to make electricity and these fuels give off harmful gases when they are burned. So try to use less electricity by turning off lights when you are not using them.
- Use products that are labeled "ozone-friendly" or "free from CFCs."
- Help to plant trees, as trees use up carbon dioxide, the main greenhouse gas.
- For short journeys, use a bicycle or walk instead of traveling by car.

Left: Acid rain can damage whole forests. It is caused by gases from factories and from car exhaust fumes mixing with water vapor in the air.

Weather Watch

Long ago, many people used "sayings" to help them remember natural signs of changes in the weather. For example, "Red sky at night, shepherd's delight" means fine weather tomorrow. It is doubtful whether these sayings work. But today, we have scientific weather forecasts based on detailed information collected from all over the world. These help weather forecasters to prepare special weather maps and to make more accurate predictions about changes in the weather.

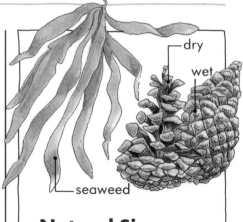

dry

wet

seaweed

Natural Signs

If rain is on the way, seaweed hung outside will feel damp, and pine cones will close up.

Weather Stations

All over the world, weather stations on land and on ships at sea continually record changing weather conditions. This photograph shows a weather station in Colorado. Balloons like this one are used to measure wind speeds. Some balloons are launched high into the atmosphere to record air pressure and temperature. Information from thousands of weather stations is sent around the world so that different countries can produce their own weather reports.

Do it yourself

Start your own weather station!

Using some of the weather instruments that you have already made, begin to keep records of the clouds, rainfall, air temperature, and air pressure in your area. You could make up symbols for different types of weather, as shown on the right.

Are your forecasts the same as those on your local television station or radio?

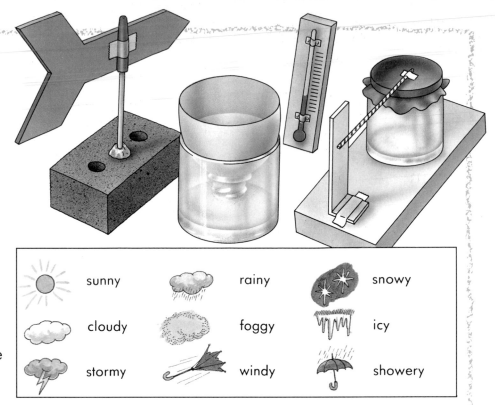

sunny		rainy		snowy	
cloudy		foggy		icy	
stormy		windy		showery	

DAY	TEMPERATURE	RAINFALL	PRESSURE	WIND	CLOUD	WEATHER SYMBOL
		0.5				

Index

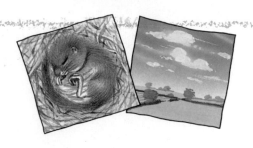